Let's Write

Reproducible Activity Sheets for Grades 4-6

Troll Associates

Copyright © 1996 by Troll Communications L.L.C.

Published by Troll Associates, an imprint and registered trademark of Troll Communications L.L.C.

All rights reserved. No part of this book may be reproduced or utilized in any form or by any means, electronic or mechanical, including photocopying, recording, or by any information storage and retrieval system, without written permission from the publisher.

Printed in the United States of America

10 9 8 7 6 5 4 3 2 1

Troll Teacher Time Savers provide a quick source of self-contained lessons and practice material, designed to be used as full-scale lessons or to make productive use of those precious extra minutes that sometimes turn up in the day's schedule.

Troll Teacher Time Savers can help you to prepare a made-to-order program for your students. Select the sequence of Time Savers that will meet your students' needs, and make as many photocopies of each page as you require. Since Time Savers include progressive levels of complexity and difficulty in each book, it is possible to individualize instruction, matching the needs of each student.

Those who need extra practice and reinforcement for catching up in their skills can benefit from Troll Teacher Time Savers, while other students can use Time Savers for enrichment or as a refresher for skills in which they haven't had recent practice. Time Savers can also be used to diagnose a student's knowledge and skills level, in order to see where extra practice is needed.

Time Savers can be used as homework assignments, classroom or small-group activities, shared learning with partners, or practice for standardized testing. See "Answer Key & Skills Index" to find the specific skill featured in each activity.

Pages 1-7 review and provide practice in identifying subjects and predicates, and recognizing and correcting sentence fragments and run-on sentences.

Pages 8-31 concentrate on the following areas of grammar: nouns, pronouns, verbs, adjectives, adverbs and prepositions.

Pages 32-51 deal with elements of punctuation and capitalization.

Pages 52-54 explore building vocabulary through the use of context clues and the dictionary.

Pages 55-72 are exercises in creative writing.

ANSWER KEY & SKILLS INDEX

Page 1, **A Strange Noise:** 1-My imaginative brother and I (subject)/heard a strange noise outside (predicate); 2-The eerie sound (subject)/seemed to float across the graveyard toward us (predicate); 3-That weird moaning and groaning noise (subject)/grew louder and louder (predicate); 4-A horrible thunderstorm (subject)/suddenly crashed down upon my brother and me (predicate); 5 through 10-Answers will vary. **(subjects & predicates)**

Page 2, **Subject & Predicate Match-Up:** 1-G; 2-D; 3-F; 4-E; 5-C; 6-I; 7-B; 8-A; 9-H; 10-J. **(subjects & predicates)**

Page 3, **Identifying Subjects & Predicates:** 1-The birds (subject)/flew higher (predicate); 2-Jessica (subject)/bought a new dress (predicate); 3-The crowd (subject)/cheered (predicate); 4-Jamal (subject)/went away (predicate); 5-We (subject)/asked Mary to go to the store (predicate); 6-The boys (subject)/were late for school (predicate); 7-The fifth grade (subject)/is going on a class trip (predicate); 8-The big, yellow bus (subject)/turned the corner (predicate); 9-the tiny tulip petal (subject)/down the stream floated (predicate); 10-Eileen (subject)/ran all the way home (predicate); 11-The tiny snowflakes (subject)/looked like shiny, white stars (predicate); 12-Tyrone and I (subject)/are going to the zoo (predicate); 13-The robot (subject)/got lost(predicate); 14-Ms. Peters (subject)/is our math teacher (predicate); 15-The siren (subject)/sounded at twelve o'clock (predicate). **(subjects & predicates)**

Page 4, **Recognizing Sentence Fragments:** 1-F; 2-S; 3-F; 4-F; 5-F; 6-S; 7-F; 8-F; 9-S; 10-F; 11-F; 12-S; 13-F; 14-S; 15-F. **(sentence fragments)**

Page 5, **Recognizing Run-On Sentences:** 1-R; 2-R; 3-S; 4-S; 5-S; 6-R; 7-S; 8-S; 9-R; 10-S; 11-R; 12-R; 13-S; 14-S; 15-R. **(run-on sentences)**

Page 6, **Recognizing Complete Sentences:** 1-F; 2-S; 3-RO; 4-F; 5-S; 6-RO; 7-F; 8-F; 9-RO; 10-RO; 11-S; 12-S; 13-F; 14-RO; 15-S. **(recognizing sentences review)**

Page 7, **Correcting Fragments & Run-Ons:** 1-fragment; 2-fragment; 3-run-on; 4-S; 5-fragment; 6-S; 7-S; 8-run-on; 9-fragment; 10-S; 11-run-on. Corrected fragments and run-ons will vary. **(correcting sentences review)**

Page 8, **Haunted Nouns:** 1-friends/house; 2-hand/face; 3-match/candle; 4-wax/floor; 5-noise/heart; 6-stairs/attic; 7-mouse/hat; 8-onion/tears; 9-ghosts/door. **(common nouns)**

Page 9, **Monkey Business:** Answers will vary. **(proper nouns)**

Page 10, **Tutti-Frutti:** 1-plums; 2-buzzes; 3-oranges; 4-dishes; 5-bunches; 6-bananas; 7-bats; 8-sixes; 9-apricots; 10-boxes; 11-guesses; 12-tangerines; 13-messes; 14-horns; 15-vines; 16-peels; 17-circuses; 18-bushes; 19-apples; 20-witches. **(plural nouns)**

Page 11, **A Survey of the City:** 1-blueberries; 2-journeys; 3-cherries; 4-fairies; 5-monkeys; 6-flies; 7-toys; 8-parties; 9-turkeys; 10-valleys; 11-ponies; 12-stories; 13-boys; 14-babies; 15-days; 16-donkeys; 17-candies; 18-keys; 19-plays; 20-ladies. **(plural nouns)**

Page 12, **Ring-A-Ding-Ding:** 1-children; 2-geese; 3-pianos; 4-halves; 5-mice; 6-oxen; 7-women; 8-shelves; 9-thieves; 10-teeth; 11-wives; 12-wolves. **(irregular plural nouns)**

Page 13, **A Secret Message:** 2-hive's; 3-boxes'; 4-woman's; 5-leaves'; 6-box's; 7-women's; 8-needle's; 9-mouse's; 10-children's; 11-geese's; 12-hives'; 13-mice's; 14-prince's; shows ownership. **(possessive nouns)**

Page 14, **Something Fishy:** 1-he; 2-they; 3-them; 4-she; 5-me; 6-her; 7-I; 8-you; 9-we; 10-it; 11-him; 12-us. **(pronouns)**

Page 15, **"There's a Frog in My Soup!":** its; their; Theirs; his; hers; her; Our; my; yours; Your; mine; Ours. **(possessive pronouns)**

Page 16, **Nouns & Pronouns:** 1-girl, station, friend (nouns)/her (pronoun); 2-school (noun)/You, I (pronouns); 3-shirt, drawer (nouns)/his (pronoun); 4-bat, ball, playground (nouns)/your (pronoun); 5-Alaska (noun)/She (pronoun); 6-Martha, olives (nouns)/I (pronoun); 7-Jell-O (noun)/We (pronoun); 8-Floyd, bicycle (nouns); 9-we, it, him (pronouns); 10-cookie (noun)/you, my, you, it (pronouns); 11-doctor, lollipop (nouns)/her (pronoun); 12-Dallas, Texas (nouns); 13-Mike, ball (nouns)/our (pronoun); 14-fair (noun)/He (pronoun); 15-honey, tea (nouns)/They, their (pronouns). **(nouns and pronouns review)**

Page 17, **Lights! Camera! Action!:** 1-rang, waited, open; 2-jangled, jumped; 3-smiled, said; 4-hurried; 5-clapped, looked; 6-filmed, announced; 7-finish; 8-raised, shouted. Answers will vary. **(action verbs)**

Page 18, **Can Dan Dive?:** 1-climb (main)/can (helping); 2-reaching (main)/should be (helping); 3-watching (main)/was (helping); 4-looking (main)/were (helping); 5-leaking (main)/had been (helping); 6-fixed (main)/must have (helping); 7-standing (main)/is (helping); 8-staring (main), are (helping); 9-dive (main)/will (helping); 10-dive (main)/did (helping); 11-dived (main)/would have (helping). **(helping verbs)**

Page 19, **Fuzzy Wuzzy:** am; is; be; was; been; are; were; are; being; was; am; was. **(verbs of being)**

Page 20, **Lizzy's Surprise:** were; tripped; laughed; have; will; had brushed; screamed; was; is; forgotten; being; are. **(verb review)**

Page 21, **Mighty Stacey:** 1-hits; 2-knocked; 3-said, am; 4-will cheer; 5-will bat; 6-promised, will slam; 7-throws, sails; 8-leans, swings; 9-struck; 10-will wear. **(verb tenses)**

Page 22, **The Contraction Factory:** 2-couldn't; 3-don't; 4-doesn't; 5-hadn't; 6-hasn't; 7-haven't; 8-isn't; 9-shouldn't; 10-wasn't; 11-weren't; 12-wouldn't; Answers will vary. **(contractions)**

Page 23, **A Knight's Fight:** Answers will vary. **(adjectives)**

Page 24, **The Spookiest Thing:** louder; loudest; quietest; scariest; spookier; taller; shakier; deepest; louder; silliest. **(comparison of adjectives)**

Page 25, **The Wrong Nail:** Answers will vary. **(adverbs)**

Page 26, **Parts of Speech Wrap-Up:** 1-names; 2-person, place, or thing; 3-proper; 4-two; 5-takes the place; 6-action; 7-together; 8-verbs of being; 9-pronoun; 10-how, when, or where. **(parts of speech review)**

Page 27, **Identifying Parts of Speech:** 1-b; 2-b; 3-c; 4-c; 5-a; 6-c; 7-a; 8-b; 9-c; 10-b. **(parts of speech review)**

Page 28, **Using Parts of Speech:** Answers will vary. **(parts of speech review)**

Page 29, **Finding Parts of Speech:** 1a-tractor, field; 1b-Bill, boys, carrots; 2a-she, him; 2b-We, it; 3a-studied; 3b-was; 4a-Big, yellow; 4b-Six, colorful; 5a-softly, carefully; 5b-Now, away. **(parts of speech review)**

Page 30, **Which Is It?:** 1-adverb, adjective; 2-verb; 3-adjective; 4-noun, verb; 5-noun, verb, adjective, noun; 6-adjective, noun, verb, adverb; 7-adjective, adverb; 8-noun, verb, noun, verb. **(words used as different parts of speech)**

Page 31, **Perry's Prepositions:** Answers will vary. **(prepositions & prepositional phrases)**

Page 32, **Capital Letters:** 1-The/Smallville; 2-Mark/I; 3-Everyone; 4-Her/Greta; 5-Greta/Columbus/Ohio; 6-She; 7-Suddenly/I/I/Greta; 8-She; 9-Mr. Dylan; 10-Everyone/Smallville. **(capitals)**

Page 33, **Time Periods:** A.M.; story.; Mr.; B.; Mrs.; G.; time.; B.C.; Mrs.; mummy.; Mr.; A.D.; 1197.; Mr.; R.; Forest.; Dr.; Sickness. **(periods)**

Page 34, **Door Prize:** 1-cross out; 2-?; 3-?; 4-cross out; 5-?; 6-cross out; 7-cross out; 8-?; 9-cross out; 10-?; 11-?; 12-cross out; 13-cross out; 14-?. **(question marks)**

Page 35, **Get the Point:** look.; is!; exclaimed.; Wow!; backyard!; happened.; slowly.; inside.; light!; Yikes!; tightly.; sky.; display!. **(exclamation points)**

Page 36, **End Marks:** 1-!; 2-?; 3-.; 4-?; 5-.; 6-!; 7-.; 8-!; 9-.; 10-!; 11-.; 12-?; 13-?; 14-!; 15-. **(end punctuation review)**

Page 37, **A Comma Drama:** 1-Mark, Dawn, Elaine,; 2-mystery,; 3- attends, ceramics, sculpture, drawing, and painting; 4-school, ceramics, sculpture,; 5-stew, pizza, macaroni and cheese, stuffed cabbage,; 6-jelly, meatloaf,; 7-balloons,; 8-drop it, kick it, punch it, beat it,. **(commas in lists)**

Page 38, **Magic Rings & Things:** 1-school, tall, thin,; 2-large,; 3-ring, it, fat,; 4-bright, colorful, coat, large,; 5-soft, warm,; 6-pudgy, said, Greetings,; 7-said, polite, voice,; 8- tattered, torn, ripped, rug, said,; 9-big, broad,; 10-landed, tiny,; 11-swirling, transparent, smoke,; 12-brief, later, disappeared,; 13-weird,. **(commas with adjectives)**

Page 39, **The Best Vacation:** 1-Say,; 2-liner,; 3-water,; 4-Indeed,; 5-fuel,; 6-Yes,; 7-However, sea,; 8-activities,; 9-For example, theaters, tennis courts,; 10-Oh,; 11-liner,; 12-Well, you,. **(comma usage)**

Page 40, **A Monstrous Tale:** 1-Myrna,; 2-door,; 3-strange, Professor Zug,; 4-Mr. Watson,; 5-you,; 6-sound, Professor,; 7-louder, isn't it,; 8-Elmo, Myrna,; 9-out, Professor,; 10-Run, everyone,. **(commas with direct address)**

Page 41, **A Big Hit:** 1-Snodgrass, singer,; 2-sister,; 3-song, Frog,"; 4-Warts," release,; 5-Ratings, town,; 6-W-I-S-H,; 7-Tomorrow, Sunday,; 8-Notes,; 9-harpsichord, instrument,; 10-Wheels,. **(commas with appositives)**

Page 42, **Good Evening:** 25,; Dracula,; Road,; Gravesend,; Saturday,; June 6,; 1982,; Street,; Tombstone,; Arizona,; Sunday,; then,. **(commas in addresses, dates, and letters)**

Page 43, **The Hardest Test in the Whole World:** 1-test.; 2-agree?; 3-is!; 4-Mrs./Edison.; 5-Ouch!; 6-short,/fast,/easy,/tests.; 7-commas,/periods,/marks,/points.; 8-Say,/test?; 9-Today,/ Friday,/test.; 10-You,/friend,/World.; 11-did?. **(punctuation review)**

Page 44, **Punctuation & Capitalization:** 1-The/today.; 2-Did/France,/England,/Spain?; 3-Larry/I/fresh,/fruit.; 4-How/was!; 5-Matthew,/Eddie,/Jason/come.;6-Get/there!; 7-Please/me.; 8-The/artists,/writers,/actors,/actresses.; 9-Where/go?; 10-Dark,/sky. **(punctuation & capitalization review)**

Page 45, **Who Said It?:** 1-"Please stop arguing with Uncle Max." (Mother); 2-"I'm not sure, but I think Julie has to be home before six o'clock." (Francine); 3-"Next time, I'll listen to your Aunt Alice." (Uncle Fred); 4-"I heard a boy call for help, so I stopped," (Aunt Doreen); 5-"I didn't take any money from Mrs. Rich," (burglar); 6-"When Grandpa was young, he had to walk more than seven miles to school every day!" (Grandma); 7-"Oh, Mrs. Giggle, I just made an awful mistake," (Maxine); 8-"Hide in the closet," (brother); 9-"If you think this is too difficult," "then raise your hand." (teacher). **(quotation marks)**

Page 46, **Could He Tell by the Smell?:** Direct quotations-I can tell by the smell; In fact, I can even sniff out a fortune whenever I want to; You're full of bologna, Dexter; If you can sniff out a fortune, let's see you do it; I will lead you to a small fortune, right here in our neighborhood; I'll find both; Look, Dad; Here come some of my friends; Give them the sugar cookies; Just like I promised; There's Freddy Fortune... Fortune. **(direct and indirect quotations)**

Page 47, **It's About Time:** Do; There's; She's; We're; I; There's; There's We're; Now; Isn't; You're; Now; Just; I; That's; My; Do. **(capitalization with quotation marks)**

Page 48, **Catch a Quote:** 1-Bugs asked, "What are you trying to catch?"; 2-Doc replied, "Oh, nothing much."; 3-"Where are you going?" asked Doc.; 4-Could Bugs have said, "I'm off to see the wizard"?; 5-Bugs exclaimed, "Watch out for that hungry lizard!"; 6-"Aha!" cried Doc as he caught the lizard.; 7-Calmly the lizard said, "I would like to have something to eat."; 8-Then Doc said, "See you later, Bugs," and he took the lizard out to lunch. **(punctuation review)**

Page 49, **A Very Silly Question:** Well; Okay; Well; Oh; Now; I; Oh. **(writing dialogue)**

Page 50, **Title Time:** 1-"Australia: The Land Down Under"; 2-The End of the World is Coming; 3-"I Have Eyes for You"/The Trivia Tabloid; 4-"Elephants Don't Wear Sneakers"; 5-"The Open Window"/Saki's Collected Short Stories; 6-The Daily Trumpet/One Lump or Two?; 7-"Are Fad Diets Good for You?"; 8-Magic Monthly. **(quotation marks in titles)**

Page 51, **Famous Quotations:** 1-...genius, Thomas Edison replied, "Genius...perspiration."; 2-"I never...future," declared A. Einstein, "for...enough."; 3-...he said, "I fear...gifts."; 4-...declared, "No...consent."; 5-"I...newspapers," said Napoleon, "more...bayonets."; 6-"Better...mind,"; 7-"There...that,". **(quotation marks review)**

Page 52, **Learning Words with Context Clues:** 1-not clear; 2-opposed; 3-enough; 4-soaked; 5-very cold; 6-sly; 7-weak; 8-well-known. **(context clues)**

Page 53, **Using the Dictionary:** 1-a; 2-a; 3-c; 4-b. **(dictionary skills)**

Page 54, **Learning Words with a Dictionary:** 1-a unit of score; 2-covered basket; 3-a flower; 4-stop the growth of; 5-a passageway, hall, or room; 6-crush; 7-a storm; 8-bright red. Answers can vary. **(context clues & the dictionary)**

Page 55, **Picture That!:** Answers will vary. **(word pictures)**

Page 56, **Idiom Ike:** 1-clumsy; 2-very happy; 3-impatient; 4-busy; 5-to have fun; 6-feeling sad; 7-pouring; 8-nervous; 9-get there before it leaves; 10-waited. **(idioms)**

Page 57, **Sound Off!:** Answers will vary. **(onomatopoeia)**

Page 58, **Two Tiny Toads:** Answers will vary. **(alliteration)**

Page 59, **Comparison Computer:** Answers will vary; 1-S; 2-M; 3-S; 4-M; 5-S; 6-S; 7-M; 8-S; 9-S; 10-S; 11-M; 12-S; 13-M; 14-M; 15-S; 16-M. **(similes & metaphors)**

Page 60, **Picture Puzzles:** Answers will vary. **(rebuses)**

Page 61, **Food Fun:** Answers will vary. **(acrostics)**

Page 62, **That's Nonsense!:** Answers will vary. **(limericks)**

Page 63, **Haiku:** Answers will vary. **(haiku verses)**

Page 64, **The Story of Me:** Answers will vary. **(writing autobiography)**

Page 65, **Step by Step:** Answers will vary. **(writing process)**

Page 66, **Scared to Death:** Answers will vary. **(descriptive writing)**

Page 67, **TV Time:** Answers will vary. **(script writing)**

Page 68, **The Jean Scene:** Answers will vary. **(writing ads)**

Page 69, **Start & Stop Stories:** Answers will vary. **(writing fiction)**

Page 70, **Story Starter:** Answers will vary. **(writing fiction)**

Page 71, **Story Ender:** Answers will vary. **(writing fiction)**

Page 70, **A Story Formula:** Answers will vary. **(fiction writing)**

Page 73, **"Just the Facts, Ma'am":** Answers will vary. **(script writing)**

Page 74, **My Hero:** Answers will vary. **(letter writing)**

Let's Write subjects & predicates

A Strange Noise

The subject of a sentence tells who or what the sentence is about.
The predicate says something about the subject.

A huge purple elephant | sat on my hat.
      subject   predicate

Jason and Tasha | gave a special gift to the teacher.
     subject   predicate

Read each sentence. Circle the subject.
Underline the predicate.

1. My imaginative brother and I heard a strange noise outside.
2. The eerie sound seemed to float across the graveyard toward us.
3. That weird moaning and groaning noise grew louder and louder.
4. A horrible thunderstorm suddenly crashed down upon my brother and me.

Add a **subject** to complete each sentence:

5. _____ looked into the graveyard.
6. _____ was coming closer and closer.
7. _____ crashed down from the sky.

Add a **predicate** to complete each sentence:

8. A glowing, misty, magical shadow
   _____.

9. My thoroughly frightened brother
   _____.

10. I _____
    _____.

Name _____ Date _____

1 Copyright © 1996 by Troll Communications L.L.C.

Let's Write | subjects & predicates

Subject & Predicate Match-Up

Match each complete subject below with the most appropriate complete predicate. Put the letter of the subject on the line.

Subjects

A. The department store

B. The fireplace

C. Her car

D. Cheesy pizzas

E. A good golfer

F. The fisherman

G. The little kitten

H. Jokes and riddles

I. The homework assignment

J. The firefighter

Predicates

1. _____ has four white paws.

2. _____ are fun to eat.

3. _____ catches herring in a net.

4. _____ putts carefully.

5. _____ stalled on the road.

6. _____ was written on the chalkboard.

7. _____ was full of ashes.

8. _____ is closed on Sundays.

9. _____ make you laugh.

10. _____ rescued the girl from the burning building.

Name_____ Date _____

Let's Write **subjects & predicates**

Identifying Subjects & Predicates

Underline the complete subject once and the complete predicate twice in each of the following sentences.

1. The birds flew higher.
2. Jill bought a new dress.
3. The crowd cheered.
4. Jamal went away.
5. We asked Mary to go to the store.
6. The boys were late for school.
7. The fifth grade is going on a class trip.
8. The big, yellow bus turned the corner.
9. Down the stream floated the tiny tulip petal.
10. Eileen ran all the way home.
11. The tiny snowflakes looked like shiny white stars.
12. Tyrone and I are going to the zoo.
13. The robot got lost.
14. Ms. Peters is our math teacher.
15. The siren sounded at twelve o'clock.

Name_____ Date_____

Let's Write   sentence fragments

Recognizing Sentence Fragments

Circle **S** after each group of words below that is a sentence. Circle **F** after each group of words below that is just a fragment.

1. An old car in the garage.   S   F
2. The car was stalled in traffic.   S   F
3. The girls in the park.   S   F
4. Written by Mark Twain.   S   F
5. When it rains.   S   F
6. When it rains, I use my umbrella.   S   F
7. Began to sink slowly down.   S   F
8. Because it was windy.   S   F
9. The teacher was thirty minutes late.   S   F
10. Studying every day.   S   F
11. Probably missed the bus.   S   F
12. I was late for school.   S   F
13. After the storm.   S   F
14. We went outside after the storm.   S   F
15. Our favorite teacher.   S   F

Name_____ Date_____

Let's Write   **run-on sentences**

Recognizing Run-On Sentences

Circle **S** after each group of words below that is a sentence. Circle **R** after each group of words below that is a run-on sentence.

1.	Dennis found out then he was happy.	S	R
2.	Don't switch the channel, I'm watching this program.	S	R
3.	Charlie ran down the hill and jumped over the fence.	S	R
4.	He slammed the door every time he walked into the room.	S	R
5.	You can play ball or go bowling.	S	R
6.	Shanna got a new comic book, it is very funny.	S	R
7.	Julie's dog follows her wherever she goes.	S	R
8.	Summer vacation is lots of fun.	S	R
9.	What do you do in the summer I go to the beach.	S	R
10.	Would you like a new kitten?	S	R
11.	Watch where you're going, you're heading for the trees!	S	R
12.	I was coming in, he was going out.	S	R
13.	Benjamin has collected lots of baseball cards.	S	R
14.	The hairy monster had three fangs and only one eye.	S	R
15.	Nobody knows where he came from he just showed up.	S	R

Name_____ Date_____

Let's Write recognizing sentences review

Recognizing Complete Sentences

Write **S** after each group of words below that is a sentence. Write **R** after each group of words that is a run-on sentence. Write **F** after each group of words below that is a fragment.

1. Sliding into first base. _____

2. Katrina discovered that she had lost her shoes. _____

3. Martin needs help can you help him? _____

4. Unless she remembers where she parked her car. _____

5. We bought some bubble gum. _____

6. Yesterday we went to your house today let's go to mine. _____

7. The best batter in the league. _____

8. Over the high picket fence. _____

9. José only ordered a soda he wasn't very hungry. _____

10. This was the best day of my life, I won the contest! _____

11. As soon as he could, he ran home. _____

12. Here they are. _____

13. Away from here. _____

14. Let's play hopscotch, I'll go first. _____

15. Susan and Maria like strawberry ice cream. _____

Name_____ Date_____

Copyright © 1996 by Troll Communications L.L.C.

Let's Write correcting sentences review

Correcting Fragments & Run-Ons

Write **S** after each group of words below that is a sentence. If a group of words is a sentence fragment, correct it on the line. If a group of words is a run-on sentence, correct it on the line.

1. José always willing to help.

2. That old piano over in the corner.

3. Be careful when you write stop when the thought is complete.

4. Sometimes everything I do turns out right.

5. Lightning flashing across the sky.

6. We could hear the thunder booming.

7. If I study hard tonight, I can pass the test tomorrow.

8. Rosa forgot her lunch money what is she going to do?

9. Running like a deer.

10. Fido found his way home.

11. The Martian is friendly, he just looks mean.

Let's Write   common nouns

Haunted Nouns

A noun is a word that names a person, place, or thing.
Something has frightened the nouns right out of these sentences. Can you put them back in the right places, so each sentence makes sense? Use each word only once.

onion match door tears hand
face floor attic
heart hat
house
noise ghosts
friends
candle stairs mouse wax

1. My _____ dared me to go into the haunted _____.

2. It was so dark that I couldn't see my _____ in front of my _____.

3. I struck a _____ and lit a _____.

4. Soon hot _____ was dripping down onto the dusty _____.

5. When I heard a strange _____, my _____ began to beat faster.

6. I tiptoed up the creaky _____ to the musty old _____.

7. Then I saw a little _____ wearing a funny _____.

8. He was eating an _____ and crying big, wet _____.

9. "There are no _____ here," I said, and I went back out the front _____.

Name_____ Date _____

Copyright © 1996 by Troll Communications L.L.C.

Let's Write — proper nouns

Monkey Business

Common nouns name people, places, or things.
Proper nouns name *particular* people, places, or things.

Morton listed some common nouns.
Can you think of a proper noun
to write next to each common noun?

Remember to start each proper
noun with a capital letter.

PEOPLE

common nouns	proper nouns
zookeeper	Simon Simian
teacher	_____
boy	_____
girl	_____
singer	_____
actor	_____

PLACES

common nouns	proper nouns
zoo	Jungleville Zoo
street	_____
city	_____
state	_____
country	_____
continent	_____

THINGS

common nouns	proper nouns
monkey	Morton
car	_____
tree	_____
song	_____
movie	_____
book	_____

Name_____ Date_____

Let's Write — plural nouns

Tutti-Frutti

A singular noun names one person, place, or thing. A plural noun names two or more persons, places, or things.

Most nouns form their plurals by adding **s** to the singular.   Example: grape — grape**s**

But nouns ending in **s, x, z, ch,** or **sh** form their plurals by adding **es** to the singular. Example: branch — branch**es**

Read each singular noun. Then write its plural form on the line.

1. plum _____
2. buzz _____
3. orange _____
4. dish _____
5. bunch _____
6. banana _____
7. bat _____
8. six _____

9. apricot _____
10. box _____
11. guess _____
12. tangerine _____
13. mess _____
14. horn _____
15. vine _____
16. peel _____
17. circus _____
18. bush _____
19. apple _____
20. witch _____

Name_____   Date_____

Let's Write   plural nouns

A Survey of the City

If a singular noun ends in Y, this is how to form the plural:

1. If the Y is preceded by a *vowel*, simply add **S** to form the plural.   Example: survey — survey**s**

2. If the Y is preceded by a *consonant*, first change the **Y** to **I**, and then add **ES** to form the plural.   Example: city — cit**ies**

Read each singular noun. Decide how the plural should be formed. Then write the plural on the line.

13. boy _____
14. baby _____
15. day _____

1. blueberry _____
2. journey _____
3. cherry   _____
4. fairy   _____
5. monkey   _____
6. fly   _____
7. toy   _____
8. party   _____
9. turkey   _____
10. valley _____
11. pony   _____
12. story   _____

16. donkey _____
17. candy _____
18. key   _____
19. play   _____
20. lady   _____

Name_____   Date_____

Let's Write — irregular plural nouns

Ring-A-Ding-Ding

The plurals of some nouns are not formed in the regular way. The dictionary will show how the plural form should be spelled.

Examples:

SINGULAR	PLURAL
man	men
foot	feet
knife	knives

Read each singular noun. Write its plural form. Use a dictionary to check your answers. How well do you think you will score?

1. child _____
2. goose _____
3. piano _____
4. half _____
5. mouse _____
6. ox _____
7. woman _____
8. shelf _____
9. thief _____
10. tooth _____
11. wife _____
12. wolf _____

How well did you score?
_____

- 12 SUPERSTAR!
- 11 STUPENDOUS
- 10 VERY GOOD
- 9 FINE
- 8 OKAY

Name _____ Date _____

Let's Write — possessive nouns

A Secret Message

The possessive case is used to show possession, or ownership.

Singular Nouns:

Most singular nouns make their possessive case by adding an apostrophe and **s**.

boy — boy's
fox — fox's

Plural Nouns:

If a plural noun already ends in **s**, make the possessive case by adding only an apostrophe.

boys — boys'
foxes — foxes'

If a plural noun does not end in **s**, make the possessive case by adding an apostrophe and **s**.

children — children's

Write the possessive case of each underlined noun. Use one space for the apostrophe, and one space for each letter. Number 1 is done for you.

1. the wing of the goose — the g o o s e ' s wing (underline under position 1: "g")
2. the queen of the hive — the _ _ _ _ _ queen (position 2)
3. the tops of the boxes — the _ _ _ _ _ _ tops (position 3)
4. the nose of the woman — the _ _ _ _ _ _ _ nose (position 4)
5. the colors of the leaves — the _ _ _ _ _ _ _ colors (position 5)
6. the bottom of the box — the _ _ _ _ _ bottom (position 6)
7. the jobs of the women — the _ _ _ _ _ _ _ jobs (position 7)
8. the eye of the needle — the _ _ _ _ _ _ _ _ eye (position 8)
9. the whiskers of the mouse — the _ _ _ _ _ _ _ whiskers (position 9)
10. the toys of the children — the _ _ _ _ _ _ _ _ _ _ _ toys (position 10)
11. the honking of the geese — the _ _ _ _ _ _ _ honking (position 11)
12. locations of the hives — the _ _ _ _ _ _ locations (position 12)
13. the tails of the mice — the _ _ _ _ _ tails (position 13)
14. the sword of the prince — the _ _ _ _ _ _ _ _ sword (position 14)

Now solve the secret message. Write the numbered letters in the correct spaces.

The possessive case _ _ _ _ _   _ _ _ _ _ _ _ _ _ .
                   1 2 3 4 5   6 7 8 9 10 11 12 13 14

Name_____ Date_____

Let's Write pronouns

Something Fishy

A pronoun is a word that is used in place of a noun.

Read the following story. Write the pronouns you would use instead of the underlined words.

Choose from the words in the box.

When Gus went fishing, <u>Gus</u> fell asleep.
                         1
All the fish saw Gus, so <u>the fish</u> did not bite the
                              2
hook. When Milly the Mermaid saw <u>the fish</u>, <u>Milly</u>
                                      3   4
said, "Listen to <u>Milly</u>." Of course the fish
                    5
listened to <u>Milly</u>. Milly said to the fish,
                6
"<u>Milly</u> will tell <u>the fish</u> what to do. <u>Milly and the fish</u>
   7   8   9
will play a trick on Gus. <u>The trick</u> will make <u>Gus</u> laugh."
                              10   11

Before long, Gus caught a big surprise, Milly. Then

all the fish laughed and said, "At least Gus

did not catch <u>the fish</u>!"
                  12

I	we
you	they
he	
she	
it	
me	us
him	them
her	

1. _____   7. _____
2. _____   8. _____
3. _____   9. _____
4. _____   10. _____
5. _____   11. _____
6. _____   12. _____

Name_____ Date_____

14   Copyright © 1996 by Troll Communications L.L.C.

Let's Write   possessive pronouns

"There's a Frog in My Soup!"

Possessive pronouns are used to show possession, or ownership.

```
my, mine
your, yours
his
her, hers
its
our, ours
their, theirs
```

My, your, his, her, its, our, and **their** are used before nouns. Example: "**Your** frog is in **my** soup."

Mine, yours, his, hers, ours and **theirs** can stand by themselves. Example: "This frog is not **mine,** so it must be **yours**!"

Read the story below. Circle the possessive pronouns you would use.

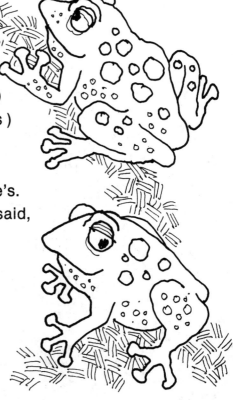

The sun had sent (its, his) warm rays down on the county fair. Now the last two entries in the frog-jumping contest picked up (their, theirs) frogs and stepped to the starting line. (Their, Theirs) were the biggest frogs in the contest. Joe held (its, his) frog, and Flo held (her, hers). Flo's eyes flashed as she looked at (her, hers) frog and at Joe's. "(Our, Ours) frogs are the biggest ones here," she said, "so they will probably be the fastest, too."

"Yes," agreed Joe, "but (my, mine) frog can out-jump (your, yours)."

"Is that so!" replied Flo. "(Your, Yours) frog doesn't stand a chance against (my, mine)."

When the contest started, all the other frogs jumped far ahead, but Joe's and Flo's sat still.

"(Our, Ours) may be the biggest frogs," laughed Flo, "but they are also the laziest!"

Name_____ Date_____

15   Copyright © 1996 by Troll Communications L.L.C.

Nouns & Pronouns

Circle all of the nouns and underline all of the pronouns in the following sentences.

1. The girl waited at the station for her friend.
2. You and I are going to school.
3. Put his shirt in the drawer.
4. Bring your bat and ball to the playground.
5. She loves to visit Alaska.
6. Martha and I like olives.
7. We also like green Jell-O.
8. Floyd wants a new bicycle.
9. Should we give it to him?
10. If you want my cookie, you can have it.
11. The doctor gave her a lollipop.
12. Dallas is in Texas.
13. What did Mike do with our ball?
14. He is going to the fair.
15. They put honey in their tea.

Let's Write   action verbs

Lights! Camera! Action!

Words that show action are called verbs.

Here are some examples: swallow, swallowed, sniff, sniffed, shake, shook.

Try to think of some action verbs that will make sense in these sentences. Write them on the lines. If you wish, you may choose from the action verbs shown in the box.

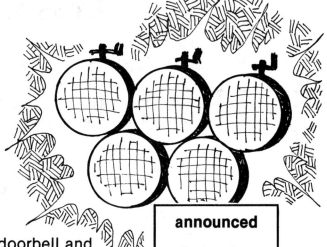

announced
clapped
filmed
finish
hurried
jangled
jumped
looked
open
raised
rang
said
shouted
smiled
waited

1. Dudley the Director _____ the doorbell and _____ impatiently for someone to _____ the door.

2. The bell _____ so loudly that Mazie almost _____ out of her skin.

3. She _____ at him and _____, "Good morning, Sir."

4. Dudley _____ inside.

5. When he _____ his hands, everyone _____ at him.

6. "Yesterday, we _____ scene two," he _____.

7. "Today, we must _____ scene three."

8. Then Dudley the Director _____ his megaphone and _____, "Lights! Camera! Action!"

Let's Write   helping verbs

Can Dan Dive?

A helping verb helps the main verb to make a statement.

In these examples, the main verb has been underlined once, and each helping verb has been underlined twice.

Has Dan climbed to the top yet?
How long has he been climbing?
Soon he will have been climbing for a whole hour!

Read each sentence. Underline the main verb once. Underline each helping verb twice.

Some common helping verbs:
am
is
are
was
were
do
does
did
have
has
had
can
will
shall
should
could
would
may
might
be
been
being
must

1. Can Dan climb all the way to the top?
2. He should be reaching the top soon.
3. At first, no one was watching him.
4. All of us were looking at that tiny tub of water at the bottom.
5. The tub had been leaking for a long time.
6. But finally, someone must have fixed it.
7. At last, Dan is standing on the platform at the top of the ladder.
8. All of us are staring at him.
9. Will he dive?
10. He did dive!
11. Would you have dived from that high platform?

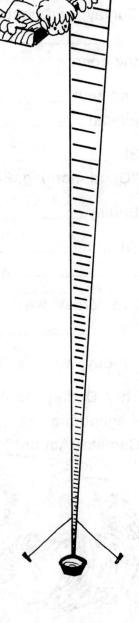

Name_____ Date_____

18   Copyright © 1996 by Troll Communications L.L.C.

Let's Write   verbs of being

Fuzzy Wuzzy

The verbs in the box below are sometimes called verbs of being.

am	was	be
is	were	being
are		been

Each sentence below is missing a verb of being. Read the choices at the end of each sentence. Write the correct *verb of being* on the line.

"I _____ too fuzzy," remarked Fuzzy Wuzzy. (am, is, are)

"My hair _____ too long," he complained. (am, is, are)

"My hair should _____ shorter!" (be, being, been)

Willy Nilly _____ Fuzzy Wuzzy's friend. (was, were)

He had _____ a barber for many years. (be, being, been)

"You _____ a lucky bear," said Willy Nilly. (am, is, are)

"Yesterday, haircuts _____ expensive," he explained. (was, were)

"But today, they _____ free!" (am, is, are)

"You are _____ silly, Willy," said Fuzzy. (be, being, been)

Soon his hair _____ much too short. (was, were)

"Look," cried Fuzzy Wuzzy, "I _____ bald!" (am, is, are)

Then Fuzzy Wuzzy wasn't fuzzy, _____ he? (was, were)

Let's Write   **verb review**

Lizzy's Surprise

Read each sentence. Look at the verbs in the box. Choose the correct verb of being, helping verb, or action verb. Write the correct verb on the line.

   Daisy and Lizzy _____ sisters.
                        (being)
One day, Daisy _____ on Lizzy's
                    (action)
roller skate. Lizzy _____ and
                         (action)
said, "I must _____ forgotten
                  (helping)
to put it away!"

   "I _____ teach her a lesson,"
         (helping)
thought Daisy. That night, when they
_____ _____ their teeth,
  (helping)   (action)
the girls climbed into their beds.

   "Eeek!" _____ Lizzy. Something
                (action)
_____ wiggling around under her
 (helping)
covers. "Ugh," she complained, "this
_____ your pet lizard!"
  (being)
   "Oh." Daisy laughed. I must have
_____ to put him away!"
   (action)
   "You are not _____ very funny,"
                       (being)
said Lizzy.

   "Now we _____ even." Daisy laughed.
                (being)

action verbs	helping verbs	verbs of being
forgotten	will	being
tripped	was	is
screamed	had	are
laughed	have	were
brushed		

Name_____   Date_____

Let's Write — verb tenses

Mighty Stacey

Verbs have tenses.
The present tense tells what is happening. ⟶ Stacey <u>plays</u> ball.
The past tense tells what has happened. ⟶ Stacey <u>played</u> ball.
The future tense tells what will happen. ⟶ Stacey <u>will play</u> ball.

Read the sentences. The missing verbs are in the box. Write the correct verbs on the lines. Make sure each verb is the right tense.

1. Stacey _____ a home run in every game.
   (present)

2. Last week, she _____ the ball right into
   (past)
   Mrs. Dandelion's greenhouse.

3. After the game, Stacey _____ to
   (past)
   Mrs. Dandelion, "I _____ sorry."
                      (present)

4. Today, I _____ for Stacey.
              (future)

5. She _____ after Gus McGoop.
         (future)

6. This morning, she _____ me, "Today,
                        (past)
   I _____ the ball over the fence."
      (future)

7. Now the pitcher _____ the ball,
                      (present)
   and now it _____ toward Stacey.
                 (present)

8. Stacey _____ back and
            (present)
   _____ with all her might!
   (present)

9. Uh-oh. Mighty Stacey just _____
                                 (past)
   out.

10. Maybe next time, she _____ her
                            (future)
    glasses.

swings
will wear
hits
throws
promised
am
will cheer
struck
knocked
leans
will slam
said
sails
will bat

Name_____ Date_____

Let's Write   contractions

The Contraction Factory

A contraction is formed when two words are joined together, and one or more letters are replaced with an apostrophe.

   Examples: did + not = didn't   was + not = wasn't

Add **not** to each of the following words to form a contraction. Write the contraction on the line. Be sure to use an apostrophe when you omit one or more letters. The first one is done for you.

1. are ____aren't____
2. could _____
3. do _____
4. does _____
5. had _____
6. has _____
7. have _____
8. is _____
9. should _____
10. was _____
11. were _____
12. would _____

Now try operating the Contraction Factory. Just combine one word from the left stack with one word from the right stack. Don't forget to add an apostrophe when you omit one or more letters.

How many contractions can you manufacture? Check your contractions in a dictionary. Three are done for you.

____he's____ _____
____he'll___ _____
____he'd____ _____
_____   _____
_____   _____
_____   _____
_____   _____

Left stack: he, she, I, you, we, they
Right stack: am, are, is, have, will, would

Name_____ Date_____

Let's Write

adjectives

A Knight's Fight

Adjectives are describing words.
They may tell which one, like **this** and **that**,
or which ones, like **these** and **those**.
They may tell what kind, like **strange**, **fast**, **gooey**, and **impossible**.
And they may tell how many, like **sixty-three**, **several**, **few**, and **many**.

Use your imagination to think of some colorful or descriptive adjectives and write them on the lines below.

1. which one _____
2. what kind _____
3. how many _____
4. what kind _____
5. what kind _____
6. how many _____
7. what kind _____
8. how many _____

9. what kind _____
10. what kind _____
11. what kind _____
12. how many _____
13. what kind _____
14. which ones _____
15. what kind _____

Now read the following story, using your adjectives in the numbered spaces.

_____1_____ knight is Sir Cedric. He is hunting for the _____2_____ dragon. It has _____3_____ _____4_____ wings, and it breathes _____5_____ fire and smoke from its _____6_____ noses. Whenever the _____7_____ beast is angry, it makes _____8_____ , _____9_____ noise(s). But Sir Cedric is _____10_____ . He knows that if he doesn't find the _____11_____ dragon, there will soon be _____12_____ more. Suddenly Cedric hears some _____13_____ sounds. He knows _____14_____ sounds. He knows that it is time for a very _____15_____ fight.

Name _____ Date _____

Let's Write **comparison of adjectives**

The Spookiest Thing

An adjective is a word that describes a noun → long   funny   strange
Many adjectives also have an -ER form → longer   funnier   stranger
            and an -EST form → longest   funniest   strangest

The -ER form is used when comparing two nouns.

The -EST form is used when comparing three or more nouns.

Monsters are **scarier** than dragons.

Ghosts are **scariest** of all.

Circle the correct form of each adjective in the story below.

    Donna heard a thump. Then she heard a thump that was (louder, loudest) than the first. The next thump was the (louder, loudest) of all. She got out of bed and moved along the hall, taking the (quieter, quietest) steps she could. There were scary shadows everywhere, but the one right behind her was the (scarier, scariest).

    "This is (spookier, spookiest) than a haunted house," she thought. A spooky shadow was following her. It was (taller, tallest) than she was. When it followed her downstairs, Donna screamed, "You can't frighten me!" But each word sounded (shakier, shakiest) than the one before. She drew in the (deeper, deepest) breath she had ever taken. That's when she heard the thumping again—and it was (louder, loudest) than it had been when she had first heard it.

    Suddenly Donna began to laugh. She felt the (sillier, silliest) she had ever felt. The thumping was the beating of her heart! And the shadow was her own!

Name_____ Date_____

Copyright © 1996 by Troll Communications L.L.C.

Let's Write

adverbs

The Wrong Nail

Adverbs are words that modify or tell about verbs. They answer the questions how? when? and where?

Sally will run fast. **How** will she run? *Fast.*
Sally will run soon. **When** will she run? *Soon.*
Sally will run outside. **Where** will she run? *Outside.*

Read the following story. Write an adverb on each line. Choose from the adverbs listed, or think up your own.

Leilani was _____ building a tree house
                     (where)
when she _____ hammered the wrong
              (how)
nail. She _____ dropped the hammer
             (when)
and _____ shouted, "Ouch!" Then
        (when)
she _____ climbed _____
       (how)   (where)
and went _____ .
              (where)
_____ she came _____ again,
    (when)   (where)
and her finger was _____ bandaged.
                          (how)
She looked _____ at the hammer and
                 (how)
the box of bright metal nails. "Next time," she

said _____ , "I will not hammer a
         (how)
*finger*nail!"

How	When	Where
neatly	soon	out
carefully	suddenly	down
cheerfully	immediately	inside
accidentally		outside
thoughtfully		

Name _____ Date _____

Let's Write   parts-of-speech review

Parts-of-Speech Wrap-Up

Use the word or words in the **Word Bank** to complete the following definitions.

Word Bank

together	action	two
how, when, or where	names	person, place, or thing
verbs of being	pronoun	takes the place
	proper	

1. A noun _____ a person, place, or thing.

2. A proper noun names a particular _____, _____, _____.

3. A _____ noun begins with a capital letter.

4. A plural noun names _____ or more persons, places, or things.

5. A pronoun _____ _____ _____ of one or more nouns.

6. A verb expresses _____ or helps to make a statement.

7. A helping verb and an action verb often work _____ .

8. "Am," "was," and "be" are called _____ .

9. An adjective is a word that describes a noun or _____ .

10. An adverb usually works with a verb to tell _____ , _____ , _____ something is done.

Name_____ Date_____

Let's Write   parts-of-speech review

Identifying Parts of Speech

Identify the part of speech of the underlined word or words in each sentence below. Circle the letter of your choice.

1. My grandmother gave me a <u>big</u> present.
   a. pronoun   b. adjective   c. verb

2. Elmo the clown <u>is</u> funny.
   a. noun   b. verb   c. adverb

3. Norman and I sat under a <u>shady</u> tree.
   a. pronoun   b. noun   c. adjective

4. Sam walked <u>slowly</u> and was late for school.
   a. verb   b. adjective   c. adverb

5. Where are <u>you</u> going?
   a. pronoun   b. noun   c. verb

6. Peter <u>jumped</u> off the stage.
   a. adjective   b. adverb   c. verb

7. The new <u>kittens</u> are on the porch.
   a. noun   b. adverb   c. pronoun

8. The player caught the ball <u>easily</u>.
   a. verb   b. adverb   c. noun

9. Carmen <u>should arrive</u> any minute.
   a. adverb   b. pronoun   c. verb

10. <u>Janet</u> found a turtle.
    a. pronoun   b. noun   c. adjective

Name_____   Date_____

27   Copyright © 1996 by Troll Communications L.L.C.

Let's Write   parts-of-speech review

Using Parts of Speech

Fill in the blanks below with a suitable word.

1. Complete each sentence by adding a **noun**.

    a. The _____ was very, very funny.

    b. Children like to play with _____ .

2. Complete each sentence by adding a **pronoun**.

    a. Is _____ coming to the meeting?

    b. _____ went to the circus.

3. Complete each sentence by adding a **verb**.

    a. Francesca _____ new clothes.

    b. The new puppy _____ all day.

4. Complete each sentence by adding an **adjective**.

    a. My hometown is _____ .

    b. Sharon met a _____ stranger.

5. Complete each sentence by adding an **adverb**.

    a. Oliver and José should arrive _____ .

    b. Felicia sings _____ .

Let's Write   parts-of-speech review

Finding Parts of Speech

Read the following sentences. Underline the correct words.

1. Underline all the **nouns** in the following sentences.

    a. The tractor stalled in the field.

    b. Bill showed the boys how to plant carrots.

2. Underline all the **pronouns** in the following sentences.

    a. Kris said she would give him an apple.

    b. We ran to see the parade when it passed.

3. Underline all the **verbs** in the following sentences.

    a. Bob studied all day.

    b. The apple was sweet and juicy.

4. Underline all the **adjectives** in the following sentences.

    a. Big, yellow flowers grow here.

    b. Six people flew colorful kites.

5. Underline all the **adverbs** in the following sentences.

    a. If you speak softly, people must listen carefully.

    b. Now they are moving away.

Name_____   Date _____

Let's Write   words used as different parts of speech

Which Is It?

Some words can be used as several different parts of speech. What part of speech a word is depends on how the word is used.

> Jean's *down* jacket was filled with   **(adjective)**
> warm *down*, or soft feathers.   **(noun)**
>
> Howard slipped and fell *down*,   **(adverb)**
> and then he rolled *down* the stairs.   **(preposition)**

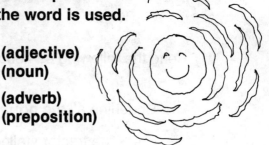

How good a detective are you? Can you figure out what part of speech each underlined word is? Write the part of speech above the word.

1. Remember to turn <u>right</u> at the <u>right</u> street.

2. Mabel tried to <u>right</u> the table that she had tipped over.

3. Because Max could eat anything, people said he had an <u>iron</u> stomach.

4. Max used a steam <u>iron</u> to <u>iron</u> his new jeans.

5. Hector is usually a <u>fast</u> runner, but today he did not score a <u>run</u> because he did not <u>run</u> <u>fast.</u>

6. A <u>weekly</u> newspaper is one that is published <u>weekly.</u>

7. If a <u>fly</u> can <u>fly,</u> can a <u>fish</u> <u>fish</u>?

Name_____   Date_____

30   Copyright © 1996 by Troll Communications L.L.C.

Let's Write

prepositions & prepositional phrases

Perry's Prepositions

A preposition is a word like *above, behind, over,* or *on.* A preposition often gives position to a noun, and is found in a prepositional phrase.

A prepositional phrase is a group of words that begins with a preposition and usually ends with a noun.
—over the rainbow
—on the dinner table

Complete each prepositional phrase below by writing a preposition on the first line, and a noun on the second line. The first one is done for you.

1. __under__ a huge, rusty __anchor__
2. _____ a funny-looking _____
3. _____ my favorite _____
4. _____ an elephant's _____
5. _____ the most wonderful _____
6. _____ Aunt Sylvia's brand-new _____
7. _____ a noisily barking _____
8. _____ fourteen smelly _____
9. _____ the third and fifth _____
10. _____ your broken _____
11. _____ Sidney's magical _____
12. _____ the thick _____
13. _____ his secret _____
14. _____ these ridiculous _____
15. _____ the highest _____

Here are some commonly used prepositions.

above
across
against
among
behind
beneath
beside
between
in
into
on
over
through
toward
under

Now turn your paper over, and use five of Perry's prepositional phrases in a sentence.

Name_____ Date_____

31

Copyright © 1996 by Troll Communications L.L.C.

Capital Letters

Rewrite the following sentences on the lines. Use capital letters wherever needed.

1. the circus came to smallville.
   _____

2. mark and i went to see it.
   _____

3. everyone was watching the trapeze star.
   _____

4. her name was greta.
   _____

5. greta came from columbus, ohio.
   _____

6. she wore a shiny, blue costume.
   _____

7. suddenly, i thought i saw greta fall.
   _____

8. she flew through the air and did a perfect triple flip.
   _____

9. mr. dylan, the ringmaster, was surprised.
   _____

10. everyone in smallville clapped.
    _____

Time Periods

**A period is used to mark the end of a statement.
Periods are also used in abbreviations.**

Rosy the Reporter left all 21 periods out of her newspaper article. Pretend you are the editor. Decide where the periods should go and insert them in Rosy's article.

    At 9:25 A M here today, two scientists told an emotion-filled story Mr B Gahn and Mrs G Willikers said that they had just returned from a journey through time They first visited Ancient Egypt in 2000 B C Mrs Willikers said she narrowly escaped being wrapped up as a mummy Mr Gahn said that he and his fellow time-traveler then went to England in A D 1197 There, they were robbed at arrowpoint by Mr R Hood of Sherwood Forest Dr Marcus Time said that both scientists were fine except for a bad case of EMOTION SICKNESS

Let's Write   question marks

Door Prize

Mark Kweschin sells only questions in his shop. But someone stole all the question marks and mixed up some statements with his questions. Can you help Mark mark the questions with question marks?

First, read each sentence. If it is a question, change the period to a question mark. If it is not a question, cross it off.

1. What we must do is wait until they unlock the door.
2. What could have made them lock it.
3. How did you get the door open so fast.
4. How I did it is no concern of yours.
5. When is a door not a door.
6. When a door is ajar (a jar), it is not a door.
7. Where Lizzy got dizzy was in the revolving door.
8. Where did Lizzy get so dizzy.
9. Whoever broke the door is going to have to pay for it.
10. Who could have knocked so hard on the door.
11. Why did the doorman throw the clock into the air.
12. Why, he wanted to see time fly, of course.
13. Will and Jill painted their front door with polka dots.
14. Will Big Otto fit in this chair.

Let's Write — exclamation points

Get the Point

A declarative sentence (a sentence that makes a statement) ends with a period.

An exclamatory sentence (a sentence that expresses strong emotion) ends with an exclamation point.

An interjection (a word that expresses emotion but is not related to any other word) is usually followed by an exclamation point.

1. George is cutting the tree down.
2. How big the tree is!
3. Ouch!

Read the following story. When you have finished reading it, go back and write the proper end mark (period or exclamation point) in each box.

    Last Fourth of July evening, Jesse heard something and went outside to take a look☐
    "How dark it is☐" she exclaimed☐
    Suddenly she cried out, "Wow☐ A flying saucer is landing right here in my backyard☐"
    She stood watching it for a long time, but nothing interesting happened☐ Finally, after about an hour, the door began to open, very slowly☐ At last, a little green man appeared and said, "Please come inside☐"
    Suddenly there was an enormous explosion and a flash of blinding light☐ "Yikes☐" screamed Jesse, covering her ears and shutting her eyes tightly☐ When she opened them again, the flying saucer was rising slowly into the night sky☐
    As she went inside, Jesse exclaimed, "What a fantastic fireworks display☐"

Name _____ Date _____

35

Copyright © 1996 by Troll Communications L.L.C.

Let's Write

end-punctuation review

End Marks

After each sentence below are three punctuation marks. Circle the one you think should end each sentence.

1. What a dreadful mess . ! ?

2. Where are your blue shoes . ! ?

3. There were four horses in the corral . ! ?

4. Are you going to Jennifer's house tonight . ! ?

5. Sarah is a Girl Scout . ! ?

6. What beautiful pictures he took . ! ?

7. Please pass the salt . ! ?

8. How tall you have grown . ! ?

9. The hippopotamus swam lazily through the water . ! ?

10. Get out of the road . ! ?

11. Dinner is on the table . ! ?

12. Who wants to set the table . ! ?

13. How much can he eat . ! ?

14. How much he has eaten . ! ?

15. We will have apple pie for dessert . ! ?

Name_____ Date_____

Let's Write   commas in lists

A Comma Drama

A comma is used to separate items in a series.
   Our drama class put on a play about ghosts, witches, goblins, and mythical monsters.

The final comma may be omitted if it is not needed to make the meaning clear.
   Our drama class put on a play about ghosts, witches, goblins and mythical monsters.

Sometimes, omitting the final comma changes the meaning of the sentence completely.
   The members of the class were put into these groups: writers, stagehands, actors, and actresses. (four groups)

   The members of the class were put into these groups: writers, stagehands, actors and actresses. (three groups)

Some pairs of words are set off as a single item.
   Before the opening night performance, I ate salad, garlic bread, *meatballs and spaghetti*, and ice cream.

If all the items in a list are separated by *and* or *or*, do not use any commas.
   I plan to be an actress *or* a lawyer *or* a plumber *or* a nuclear physicist.

Read the sentences below. Add commas where they are needed.

1. Mark Dawn Elaine and Danny met us at the movies.

2. We could not decide whether to see a comedy or a mystery musical or a drama.

3. At the art school she attends Mary Jane received A's in these four subjects: ceramics sculpture drawing and painting.

4. At another art school her cousin received A's in these three subjects: ceramics sculpture drawing and painting.

5. My favorite meals are stew pizza macaroni and cheese stuffed cabbage and roast turkey.

6. My three favorite sandwiches include the following: peanut butter and jelly meatloaf and bologna.

7. The room was filled with toys and games and balloons and people who were having lots of fun.

8. The salesperson said, "You can't break this, even if you drop it kick it punch it beat it and stomp on it."

Magic Rings & Things

When two or more adjectives are used in a series, they should be separated by commas. (Do not use a comma after the last adjective in the series.)

example: This is a **wild, unbelievable, impossible, silly** story.

Read each sentence. Add commas where they are needed. Each sentence will need at least one comma.

1. On my way to school, I met a tall thin mysterious boy.

2. He wore a large shiny ring on his finger.

3. It must have been a magic ring, because when he rubbed it, a fat wonderful genie suddenly appeared.

4. He wore a bright colorful polka-dot coat, and a large circular ring in his ear.

5. On his feet were soft warm fuzzy slippers.

6. He held out his pudgy pink hands and said, "Greetings, Master."

7. My new friend said, in a polite confident voice, "We would like a ride on a magic carpet."

8. So the genie brought out a tattered torn ripped ragged rug, and said, "Hop right on!"

9. Then he took us on a fantastic ride all around the big broad beautiful land.

10. When he landed, my friend took out a tiny magical box.

11. Suddenly there was a puff of swirling transparent purple smoke, and the genie instantly disappeared.

12. A brief silent moment later, my new friend disappeared, too.

13. I never saw those weird wonderful strangers again.

Let's Write — commas in compound sentences and commas with introductory words

The Best Vacation

A comma should be used before *and, but, or, nor,* and *for* (meaning "because") when these words join the parts of a compound sentence.

> The travel agent is overweight, but he will not try to lose any pounds.
>
> He will not go on a diet, for he loves to munch on peanuts all day.

A comma is also used after introductory words like *oh, well, yes, say, however, indeed,* and *for example.*

> Indeed, he eats six hundred bags of peanuts every single day!

Read each sentence below, and add the comma where it belongs.

1. Say why don't you forget about going to the mountains on your vacation this year?
2. Wouldn't you like to sail around the world on an ocean liner or wouldn't you like to take a round-the-world cruise in a submarine?
3. A submarine can go deep down in the water but it can't carry too many passengers.
4. Indeed some submarines can carry only one or two people.
5. Some submarines use nuclear fuel and they can sail all the way around the world without refueling.
6. Yes a submarine ride would be an interesting way to spend your vacation.
7. However you may prefer to sail on the surface of the sea instead of down near the bottom of the ocean.
8. Ocean liners can offer many different kinds of activities for they are so much larger than submarines.
9. For example ocean liners have movie theaters tennis courts and even swimming pools.
10. Oh I didn't realize that you always get seasick.
11. You probably shouldn't take a cruise on an ocean liner nor should you go aboard a submarine.
12. Well maybe a vacation in the mountains is best for you after all!

Name_____ Date_____

Let's Write   commas with direct address

A Monstrous Tale

Commas are used to set off names used when speaking directly to someone.

I'm sorry, my good man, but we don't allow monsters in here.

Bolt the door, Myrna!

Elmo, make sure the windows are closed and locked.

Read the sentences below. Decide who is being spoken to. Then use commas to set off their names or the words that are used to address them directly.

1. Myrna it will be your job to guard the front door.

2. Keep an eye on the back door Elmo.

3. If you hear anything strange Professor Zug be sure to let us know.

4. Mr. Watson please turn that noisy radio off.

5. Thank you sir.

6. Do you hear a weird sound Professor coming from just outside the laboratory?

7. It's getting louder, isn't it my friends?

8. Elmo take Watson and Myrna, and find out what's going on.

9. Watch out Professor the monster is coming in through the window!

10. Run everyone run for your lives!

Let's Write — commas with appositives

A Big Hit

A word or words used to identify or explain a noun or pronoun should be set off by commas.

The guitar, my favorite instrument, has six strings.

My favorite song, "Big Boy," is about a man who swallows a whole watermelon.

Read the following sentences, and decide which word or words should be set off by commas. Then add the commas where they are needed.

1. Velma Snodgrass the well-known singer has just released a new song.

2. She is accompanied by her equally famous sister Vera Snodgrass.

3. Velma's last song "I Kissed a Frog " was a big hit.

4. "Warts " her new release is bound to reach the top ten.

5. Arlo Ratings the most popular disc jockey in town plays Velma's new song every day.

6. Arlo has a three-hour show on W-I-S-H the local radio station.

7. Tomorrow Sunday he will play all the songs Velma ever recorded.

8. Each song was written by Lotta Notes a famous songwriter.

9. Lotta uses the harpsichord a keyboard instrument when she writes her songs.

10. I think Lotta also writes songs for *Hub Cap and the Four Wheels* that famous singing group.

Name_____ Date_____

Let's Write — commas in addresses, dates, and in letters

Good Evening

Commas are used in dates to separate days, months, and years.

Commas are used in addresses to separate apartment numbers, streets, cities, and states.

Commas are also used after the greeting and closing in personal letters, and after the closing in business letters.

Study the way the commas are used in the letter below.

July 21, 1982

Dear Miss Fortune,

I was born on Friday, March 13, 1406, in Transylvania. Recently I moved to an apartment in your country. If you will come to 4256 Vampire Lane, Apartment 16B, Great Neck, New York, I will be pleased to bite you on the neck!

Very truly yours,

Count Dracula

Now read the following letter, and insert the missing commas.

July 25 1982

Dear Count Dracula

I cannot come to your apartment in Great Neck because I am vacationing at 16 Cemetery Road Gravesend California. I arrived on Saturday June 6 1982 and I will be here all summer. I will return to my winter home at 1507 Plasma Street Tombstone Arizona on Sunday August 31. Until then, I will see you in my dreams.

Affectionately

Iva Fortune

Let's Write — review: periods, question marks, exclamation points, and commas

The Hardest Test in the Whole World

Eddie the Editor says this is the hardest test in the whole world. He says that anyone who can finish it is a first-class, number one punctuation prodigy.

You see, Eddie removed the periods, question marks, and exclamation points from the following sentences. He also removed the commas. Can you put all the periods, question marks, exclamation points, and commas back?

1. Eddie says that this is a hard test

2. Do you agree

3. How difficult it is

4. This test was made up by Mrs Edith Edison

5. Ouch

6. Some people only like short fast easy enjoyable tests

7. Some people don't like tests that ask about things like commas periods question marks and exclamation points

8. Say why don't you try to get a perfect score on this test

9. Today Friday is the last day you can take this test

10. You my friend have almost finished The Hardest Test in the Whole World

11. How do you think you did

Name_____ Date_____

Let's Write **punctuation & capitalization review**

Punctuation & Capitalization

Rewrite the following sentences on the lines. Use capital letters and punctuation marks wherever they are needed.

1. the teacher was not in school today
   _____

2. did you visit france england and spain
   _____

3. larry and i like fresh sweet fruit
   _____

4. how scary that movie was
   _____

5. matthew eddie and jason all want to come
   _____

6. get down from there
   _____

7. please open the door for me
   _____

8. the four groups are artists writers actors and actresses
   _____

9. where do we go
   _____

10. dark gloomy clouds filled the sky
    _____

Name_____ Date _____

Let's Write   **quotation marks**

Who Said It?

Quotation marks are used to set off a quotation—a speaker's exact words.

The teacher said, "Did I hear someone laugh, or was it my imagination?"

Father said, "Have a good time," as he waved good-by.

Later, he asked, "Did you have a good time?"

Read each sentence. Add quotation marks to set off the speaker's exact words. Then, on the line, tell who said it.

1. Mother said, Please stop arguing with Uncle Max. _____

2. Francine said, I'm not sure, but I think Julie has to be home before six o'clock. _____

3. Uncle Fred moaned, Next time, I'll listen to your Aunt Alice. _____

4. I heard a boy call for help, so I stopped, declared Aunt Doreen. _____

5. I didn't take any money from Mrs. Rich, insisted the burglar. _____

6. Grandma laughed and said, When Grandpa was young, he had to walk move than seven miles to school every day! _____

7. Oh, Mrs. Giggle, I just made an awful mistake, wailed Maxine. _____

8. My brother said, Hide in the closet, so that's exactly what I did. _____

9. If you think this is too difficult, said the teacher, then raise your hand. _____

Let's Write — direct & indirect quotations

Could He Tell by the Smell?

Quotation marks are used to set off *direct quotations* **— the speaker's exact words.** ⟶ When Walter heard me say, "My car won't start," he was kind enough to say I could borrow his car.

Quotation marks are *not* used to set off *indirect quotations*. ⟶

Read the following story. Decide if the underlined words are direct quotations or indirect quotations. Use quotation marks to set off the direct quotations.

    Dexter always said <u>he could tell when he was near money</u>. <u>I can tell by the smell</u>, he bragged. <u>In fact, I can even sniff out a fortune whenever I want to</u>.

    Dexter's friends said <u>he was making things up</u>. <u>You're making things up, Dexter,</u> they said. <u>If you can sniff out a fortune, let's see you do it!</u>

    Dexter said <u>he would be glad to</u>. <u>I will lead you to a small fortune, right here in our neighborhood</u>, he said. Everyone said <u>they would be happy with a small fortune, but a big fortune would be better</u>. Dexter said, <u>I'll find both</u>.

    Dexter started crawling along and sniffing. Everyone followed him.

    Soon Freddy looked out the window of Fortune's Bakery. <u>Look, Dad</u>, he said. <u>Here come some of my friends</u>.

    Freddy's father said <u>Freddy could give one cookie to each of his friends</u>. <u>Give them the sugar cookies</u>, he added.

    Dexter stopped sniffing at the bakery door. <u>Just like I promised</u>, he said. <u>There's Freddy Fortune and his father. That's a small Fortune and a big Fortune</u>!

"The nose knows."

It's About Time

Capitalize the first word of a direct quotation.

➡ "Where are we?" whispered Sue. Tammy replied, "We're in my time machine."

Do not capitalize the second part of a quoted sentence that is interrupted by words like *she said*.

➡ "If you'll look closely," she added, "you'll see that we're traveling through time."

Each new sentence, of course, begins with a capital letter.

➡ "This is great!" exclaimed Sue. "We're passing through the 19th century! It's fascinating!"

Read the following story. Circle the letters that should be capitalized.

Sue stared out the window of the time machine. "do I really see," she asked, "what I think I see?"

"there's Becky Thatcher," said Tammy. "she's lost in the cave with Tom Sawyer." Then Tammy added, "we're still moving back through time."

"i believe," interrupted Sue, "that we're in the 18th century now. there's Robinson Crusoe, shipwrecked on his island."

A few minutes later, Tammy said, "there's Don Quixote, tilting at windmills. we're obviously in the 1600's."

"now we must be passing through the 1100's," cried Sue. "isn't that Robin Hood," she asked, "over there in Sherwood Forest?"

"you're right," agreed Tammy. "now, however," she added, "it's time for us to return to the present. just press that little red button."

Suddenly the time machine turned and raced through the centuries. Soon they had stopped in the twentieth century.

"if you'll meet me here at midnight," said Tammy, "we can do this again."

"that's a great idea," agreed Sue. "my watch, however," she quickly added, "seems to have stopped. do you have the time?"

Let's Write

commas, question marks, exclamation points and periods with direct quotations

Catch a Quote

Here are five rules for punctuating direct quotations:

1. Separate a direct quotation from the rest of the sentence by using commas, a question mark, or an exclamation point.
2. Use only one punctuation mark at the end of a quotation.
3. If a period or a comma is used, place it inside the closing quotation marks.
4. If a question mark or exclamation point is used, place it inside the closing quotation marks if the quotation is a question or exclamation.
5. If a sentence is a question or exclamation, but the quotation is not, the question mark or exclamation point is placed outside the closing quotation marks.

Now study these examples:

Marty announced, "I'm leaving now," and he left.
Mary asked, "Are you coming?" and she walked out.
Manny shouted, "Good-by!" as he slammed the door.
Molly said, "You should have been more polite."
Morty asked, "Do you think they'll come back?"
Did anyone hear Mindy say, "They'll be back"?
Micky shouted, "They'll never be back!"
How happy Maggie was when Moe said, "Please come in"!

Now add the commas, periods, question marks, and exclamation points to the following sentences.

1. Bugs asked   "What are you trying to catch "
2. Doc replied   "Oh, nothing much "
3. "Where are you going " asked Doc
4. Could Bugs have said   "I'm off to see the wizard"
5. Bugs exclaimed   "Watch out for that hungry lizard "
6. "Aha " cried Doc   as he caught the lizard
7. Calmly the lizard said   "I would like to have something to eat "
8. Then Doc said   "See you later, Bugs " and he took the lizard out to lunch

Name_____ Date_____

Let's Write

quotation marks in dialogue

A Very Silly Question

Dialogue is conversation between two or more people. **When you write dialogue, you should indent each time the speaker changes.**

> "What happened here?" asked the police officer.
> "There's been an accident," replied the driver.
> "I can see that," said the police officer. "How did it happen?"
> "It wasn't my fault, Officer," insisted the driver. "I beeped my horn, but the tree wouldn't move!"

Read the following conversation between Julie and Mark. Circle each word that should begin a new paragraph. The first three have been done for you.

"(Hello), Mark," said Julie. "(Hi)," Mark replied, sitting down next to her. "I have a question for you, Julie." "(Go) ahead," said Julie, smiling. "Well," Mark began, "suppose two cars are driving in opposite directions on a highway. One car is heading toward Kansas, and the other one is headed toward Colorado." "Okay," agreed Julie. "What happened next, Mark?" "Well, when the cars reach the border that separates Kansas from Colorado," continued Mark, "they crash into each other." "Oh, no!" cried Julie. "How awful!" "Now, my question," concluded Mark, "is this: If the accident happened right on the state line, in which state would you bury the survivors?" "I guess," replied Julie, "I'd bury half in Kansas, and half in Colorado. Where would *you* bury the survivors, Mark?" "Oh," laughed Mark, "I guess that since they're *survivors,* I wouldn't bury them at all!"

Name_____ Date_____

Let's Write

Title Time

quotation marks in titles

Use quotation marks to set off the titles of short poems, songs, short stories, chapters, and episodes of TV shows.
Use italics for (or underline) the titles of books, plays, newspapers, magazines, TV series, and movies.

The article "Should Vampires Wear Braces?" appeared in a recent issue of the magazine *Overbite,* which I was reading yesterday in the orthodontist's office.

Add the correct punctuation (quotation marks or underlining) to the following sentences.

1. Our teacher asked everyone to read the last chapter, entitled Australia: The Land Down Under, in our geography book.

2. Throckmorton J. Doomsday is writing a new book called The End of the World Is Coming.

3. The hit song, I Have Eyes for You, was written by a potato farmer, according to the weekly newspaper called The Trivia Tabloid.

4. My favorite poem is Elephants Don't Wear Sneakers.

5. The Open Window is my favorite story in a book called Saki's Collected Short Stories.

6. According to The Daily Trumpet, which is my home town newspaper, that new play entitled One Lump or Two? is going to be a big hit.

7. Have you read this feature article called Are Fad Diets Good for You?

8. I looked for the latest issue of my favorite magazine, Magic Monthly, but it had disappeared!

Name_____ Date_____

50 Copyright © 1996 by Troll Communications L.L.C.

Let's Write

review:
quotation marks &
commas in quotations

Famous Quotations

Each of the following sentences contains at least one direct quotation. But Meddlesome Mark has taken the quotation marks out. He has also removed the commas that should separate each quotation from the rest of the sentence in which it appears.

Read each sentence. Add the necessary quotation marks and commas.

1. When he was asked to define *genius* Thomas Edison replied Genius is one percent inspiration and ninety-nine percent perspiration.

2. I never think of the future declared Albert Einstein for it comes soon enough.

3. When a wise Trojan saw that the departing Greek army had left a huge wooden horse outside the walls of Troy he said I fear the Greeks even when they offer gifts.

4. In 1854 Abraham Lincoln gave a speech in which he declared No man is good enough to govern another man without that other's consent.

5. I fear three newspapers said Napoleon more than a hundred thousand bayonets.

6. Better an ugly face than an ugly mind quipped James Ellis.

7. There I guess King George will be able to read that announced John Hancock as he signed the Declaration of Independence.

Name_____ Date_____

Let's Write   context clues

Learning Words with Context Clues

Circle the word or words that mean about the same as the underlined word in each sentence below. Use context clues to help you figure out the meaning of the underlined words.

1. Marlene gave a <u>vague</u> answer, one that was not clear at all.

   not answered　　　　not clear　　　　not friendly

2. His unusual ideas are <u>contrary</u> to everyone else's.

   opposed　　　　similar　　　　used

3. The water in the canteen was <u>sufficient</u> to last us all day.

   heavy　　　　enough　　　　empty

4. The heavy rain completely <u>saturated</u> the front lawn.

   weeded　　　　soaked　　　　dried out

5. Ron thought he was going to a <u>frigid</u> place, but it was actually very hot.

   very hot　　　　far away　　　　very cold

6. The <u>cunning</u> thief used many tricks to get what he wanted.

   sly　　　　lazy　　　　hungry

7. My old dog Wheeler is too <u>feeble</u> to run anymore.

   strong　　　　short　　　　weak

8. That doctor is very <u>prominent</u>, or well-known, in his field.

   well-known　　　　proper　　　　interested

Name_____ Date _____

Let's Write   dictionary skills

Using the Dictionary

Look up each underlined word below in the dictionary. Then circle the correct ending to each of the following sentences.

1. The word <u>fortune</u> means _____
   - a. luck
   - b. your future
   - c. talent
   - d. all of the above

2. The word <u>magazine</u> can mean a _____
   - a. military warehouse
   - b. paper mill
   - c. lantern
   - d. none of the above

3. A <u>spoonbill</u> is a _____
   - a. special spoon
   - b. leaflet
   - c. bird
   - d. fish

4. If you had a <u>yawl</u>, you would _____
   - a. eat it
   - b. sail on it
   - c. fly on it
   - d. read it

Name_____ Date _____

Let's Write   **context clues & the dictionary**

Learning Words with a Dictionary

In each sentence below, one word has been underlined. Some of the underlined words have more than one meaning. Use the dictionary to get the exact definition for each underlined word as it is used in the sentence. Write the definition on the line.

1. Francine made the winning point.
   _____

2. Our picnic hamper will hold all of this food.
   _____

3. A sweet-smelling pink is growing in the garden.
   _____

4. Overwatering will stunt the plant's growth.
   _____

5. Harry met Greg in the vestibule of the building.
   _____

6. Bertha can squash a soda can with one hand.
   _____

7. We watched from the window as a squall hit the beach.
   _____

8. The new carpet was crimson.
   _____

Name _____ Date _____

Let's Write   word pictures

Picture That!

Some words can be written to look like what they mean. In the space below, design your own word pictures. Choose words from the list, or think of some of your own.

WORD LIST

fire	slide	scary	cut	top	down
up	eyes	bounce	wet	curly	jagged
wheel	jump	broken	circle	sad	tiny
wide	diamond	narrow	round	pump	square

Name_____ Date_____

Let's Write   idioms

Idiom Ike

Ike likes to use idioms when he talks. **An *idiom* is a group of words that has a special meaning when they are used together.** Ike doesn't really mean that Mike should put his eye on the bicycle. He means that Mike should *watch* the bike.

Draw lines to match the idioms on the left with their meanings on the right.

1. I'm *all thumbs*.   feeling sad

2. She's *walking on air*.   busy

3. They're *itching to go*.   to have fun

4. She's *tied up right now*.   clumsy

5. They did it *just for kicks*.   very happy

6. He's *down in the dumps*.   impatient

On the lines below, write what each of the following idioms mean. Then for fun, turn the paper over and draw a picture to show the literal, or word-for-word, meaning of one idiom.

7. It's raining cats and dogs._____

8. My stomach is tied up in knots. _____

9. I have to catch a bus. _____

10. She stuck around until three-thirty. _____

Can you think of other idioms? Write them here.

_____

_____

_____

Name_____ Date _____

56   Copyright © 1996 by Troll Communications L.L.C.

Let's Write **words & sounds**

Sound Off!

Some words sound like what they describe. For example, say the word *buzz* out loud. Doesn't it sound like the sound a bee makes?

Think of the meaning of each word below. Then read the words out loud. Listen to their sounds. Choose five of the words and use each one in a sentence.

screech	hiss	pop	sizzle	whoosh	crack
slosh	choppy	hum	purr	zip	cuckoo

1. _____
   _____
2. _____
   _____
3. _____
   _____
4. _____
   _____
5. _____
   _____

Can you think of other words that sound like what they describe? Write them here.

_____
_____

Name_____ Date _____

Let's Write  alliteration

Two Tiny Toads

Alliteration is the repetition of words that begin with the same letter or sound.

For example:

Two tiny toads took a taxi.

Brian brought brownies for his brother Bruce.

Start a sentence with each one of the words below. Try to make all or most of the words in each sentence begin with the same sound. You may use a dictionary or a thesaurus to help you.

1. Dull _____
2. Five _____
3. Great _____
4. Little _____
5. Stanley _____

On the lines below, write a paragraph, a poem, or several unrelated sentences. Use the same sound to start as many words as possible.

_____
_____
_____
_____
_____
_____
_____
_____
_____
_____

Name_____ Date_____

Copyright © 1996 by Troll Communications L.L.C.

Let's Write   similes/metaphors

Comparison Computer

The computer is stumped! Can you complete the similes and metaphors below?

A *simile* is a figure of speech that compares *unlike* things by using the words *like* or *as*:

  The sharpened pencil is as pointy as a nail.

A *metaphor* is a figure of speech that compares unlike things, but does *not* use the words *like* or *as*:

  A motorboat is a water rocket.

After you have completed the following sentences, label them. Write an **S** on the line after the sentence if it is a simile. Write an **M** on the line after the sentence if it is a metaphor.

1. The motor was as quiet as _____. ____
2. Red is _____. ____
3. The ride was as bumpy as _____. ____
4. A whisper is _____. ____
5. It is round like _____. ____
6. Shopping is as dull as _____. ____
7. A caterpillar is _____. ____
8. She jumped like _____. ____
9. Her eyes were like _____. ____
10. Barbara's sheepdog is as big as _____. ____
11. A flower is _____. ____
12. He sang like _____. ____
13. The sky is _____. ____
14. Clouds are _____. ____
15. Carla's new shoes are as slippery as _____. ____
16. Rain is _____. ____

Name_____ Date _____

Let's Write rebuses

Picture Puzzles

A *rebus* is a kind of puzzle. It uses pictures and symbols in place of words or parts of words to make sentences. For example:

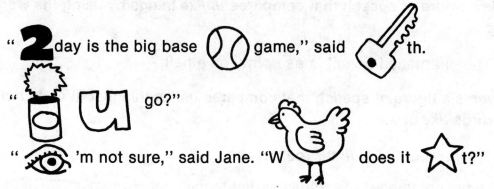

Make up a rebus story. Use at least ten symbols. Use the symbols on this page or think of some symbols of your own.

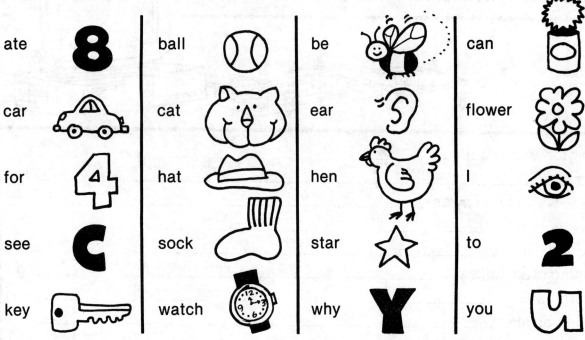

Write your story here:

_____
_____
_____
_____
_____

Name_____ Date_____

Let's Write — acrostics

Food Fun

What's your favorite food? Write an acrostic about it. **An *acrostic* is a poem in which certain letters, usually the first letter of each line, form a word or message when these letters are read in sequence.** First, write the food name in capital letters down the side of your paper. Then use each letter to begin a word or phrase that tells something about the food.

For example: SPAGHETTI   Write yours here.

Slippery, squiggly   _____

Pasta   _____

Absolutely the best   _____

Great with gravy   _____

Healthful and delicious   _____

Everyone enjoys   _____

Tastes great   _____

Twisted or straight   _____

It's my favorite!   _____

Now on the back of this paper, try writing an acrostic for a person, animal, color, sport, or anything else you'd like.

Name_____ Date _____

Let's Write   limericks

That's Nonsense!

There once was a fellow from Knox,
Whose hobby was searching for rocks.
    Although that's not bad,
    It made his mom mad
'Cause he kept them inside his socks.

A *limerick* is a humorous or nonsense verse. Read the limerick above. Which lines rhyme? Read it again, out loud, This time, listen for the rhythm as you read. When you have a feel for the rhythm pattern and the rhyme scheme, write your own limericks on the lines below.

There once was a _____

Who liked to _____

_____

_____

_____

_____

_____

_____

_____

Name_____ Date _____

Let's Write

haiku verses

Haiku

A *haiku* is a kind of Japanese poem. It has three short lines—often with five syllables, seven syllables, and five syllables.
A haiku is usually about something in nature, especially the seasons.

The autumn leaves fall—
Red, yellow, orange and brown
Crunch beneath my feet.

The tulip in spring—
Slow, quiet, it awakens
From its winter sleep.

Try writing your own haiku verses. If you like, illustrate them, too.

_____

_____

_____

_____

_____

_____

Name_____ Date _____

Let's Write

writing autobiography

The Story of Me

Write an *autobiography*—a story about yourself. Draw pictures or paste on photographs to help illustrate your story. The headings and questions below will give you some ideas about what to write. Use the back of this page if you need more space.

1. <u>Meet Me!</u> What is your name? How did you get your name? How old are you? When and where were you born?

2. <u>Family Tree</u>. Who are the members of your family? What are they like? Where do you live? What is your home like?

3. <u>The Three R's</u>. Where do you go to school? Describe your school, class, teachers, and favorite subjects.

4. <u>Friends to the End</u>. Who are your friends. What do you like best about them? What do you like least?

5. <u>Just for Fun</u>. What are your hobbies and interests?

6. <u>Like It or Not.</u> What are some things you like and dislike? Why?

7. <u>It's the Most!</u> What are the most exciting, embarrassing, and frightening things that have ever happened to you? Describe them.

8. <u>Feelings</u>. What are some things that make you happy? sad? angry? lonely? frightened? excited? satisfied?

9. <u>Crystal Ball</u>. What do you think you will be like in five years? In fifteen years?

_____
_____
_____
_____
_____

Name_____ Date_____

Let's Write

writing process

Step by Step

Writing is a process, which means it develops in stages. First, you must decide what to write about. One way to do this is to jot down some ideas or discuss them with someone. This first stage is called *prewriting*. Then you organize your ideas and write them down. That's called *drafting*. The third stage is *revising*. That's where you go back to improve your first draft by making it easier to understand and improving the organization. Stage 4 is called *editing*, and it includes checking for mistakes in grammar, punctuation, and spelling.

Going through these 4 stages, prepare a paragraph giving your opinion on an important issue. Check off each stage as you complete it.

☐ Stage 1: Put down some thoughts as they occur to you. Discuss them with others. Choose your topic.

_____

_____

_____

_____

☐ Stage 2: Put your thoughts together in a logical sequence. Write a first draft on the back of this paper.

☐ Stage 3: Go over your draft. Is it clear? Do you need to explain more in some places? Does one sentence lead logically to the next? Make all the changes necessary to make your paragraph stronger and clearer. Rewrite on another piece of paper.

☐ Stage 4: Go over your second draft and check for mistakes in spelling and punctuation. Do all the sentences begin with capital letters? Look for sentence fragments and run-ons too. Now rewrite your paragraph for the last time.

Now it's time to share your work. Congratulations on a job well done, writer.

Name_____ Date_____

Let's Write   descriptive writing

Scared to Death

Describing how a place looks, sounds, smells, and feels can make that place seem real to the reader. Descriptive words and phrases that appeal to the reader's senses are the most effective. "Clammy" is better than "cool," for instance, and "the spicy-sweet smell of apple pie" is better than "the aroma of baking."

In the space below, write a description of the scariest place you've ever been. It might be a haunted house or your own room. It might be an imaginary place, too. Use sensory words to make the place seem real. Here are a few examples: shadowy, screech, hoarse, inky darkness, foul odor. Make a list of words and phrases that describe your scary spot.

_____

_____

_____

_____

_____

Now use those words and phrases in a descriptive paragraph. Continue on the back if you need more room.

_____

_____

_____

_____

_____

_____

_____

_____

_____

Name_____ Date_____

Let's Write   script writing

TV Time

Suppose you have been hired to write a new TV show. Think about the kind of show you'd like to write. Then use your imagination to fill in the answers below.

What kind of show will you write (comedy, music, drama, game show)?
_____

What age group of people will the show appeal to most? _____

What will the show be called? _____

Describe the setting. _____
_____
_____

Name and describe the characters or contestants. _____
_____
_____
_____

Write an outline or several paragraphs to summarize the story or events. Or, if you like, write the script in dialogue form. Continue on the back of this page.
_____
_____
_____
_____
_____
_____
_____
_____
_____

Name _____   **Date** _____

Let's Write writing ads

The Jean Scene

A famous clothing designer has just come out with a new pair of jeans. It's your job to give the jeans a name and write a short TV commercial to advertise them. The commercial should make viewers want to rush out to buy the jeans.

What will the commercial look like? Describe the setting. Will there be actors and actresses, singers and dancers? What will they be doing?

_____
_____
_____
_____
_____
_____
_____
_____

How will the commercial start? How will it end? What will the commercial say? Write the jingle or dialogue here.

_____
_____
_____
_____
_____
_____
_____
_____

Name_____ Date_____

Let's Write   **writing fiction**

Start & Stop Stories

Pick a story starter from the first list and a story stopper from the second list. They do not have to be related to each other in any way. Now fill in the middle of the story with the plot and details. Draw a picture to go with your story.

STORY STARTERS

1. Last night I had the most unusual dream.
2. Today is the big day!
3. As I walked past the old deserted house, I heard strange noises coming from inside.
4. I always thought my computer was my friend. But one day...

STORY STOPPERS

1. They all laughed until their sides hurt.
2. She found a friend, after all.
3. He wagged his tail, and I knew he was happy to see me.
4. And that's how the mystery was solved. Of course, I knew who did it all along.

_____
_____
_____
_____
_____
_____
_____
_____
_____
_____
_____
_____

Name_____ Date_____

Let's Write — writing fiction

Story Starter

Use your imagination to complete the story below. You have been given the beginning of the story. Be sure to give your story a title. If you like, draw a picture to illustrate it on the back of this page.

title: _____

by _____

   It was a gloomy, rainy day. My best friend and I were just sitting around wishing something exciting would happen. Suddenly, we heard a loud crash—and then a screech! _____

_____
_____
_____
_____
_____
_____
_____
_____
_____
_____
_____
_____
_____
_____
_____
_____

Name _____ Date _____

Let's Write ... **writing fiction**

Story Ender

Use your imagination to complete the story below. You have been given the ending of the story. Be sure to give your story a title. If you like, draw a picture to illustrate it on the back of this page.

title: _____

by _____

_____
_____
_____
_____
_____
_____
_____
_____
_____
_____

"At last." Jessica smiled. "I thought you'd disappeared."

Name _____ Date _____

Let's Write

writing fiction

A Story Formula

Good stories have certain things in common. Each story has
1. a made-up main character
2. something the character wants or needs
3. an obstacle, something that prevents the character from having what he or she wants
4. a resolution, or way around the obstacle

Choose one thing from each group and write a story that includes your four choices. Use the back of this page if you need more space.

Main Character
Dave, a great soccer player
Becky, who loves to dance
Amanda, who is hearing impaired
José, an amateur astronomer

What He or She Wants
a new telescope
a special ring
ballet camp
a good friend

Obstacle
Mom loses her job
a new kid in class
Dad hates sports
a broken leg

Resolution
help someone learn to skate
help to sew costumes
Mom has some money saved
show responsibility

Title: _____

_____
_____
_____
_____
_____
_____
_____
_____
_____
_____

Name _____ Date _____

Let's Write   **script writing**

"Just the Facts, Ma'am"

What if you were the head writer of your favorite TV cop show? Make up a story for the show in which a mystery is solved. Be sure there is a beginning, middle, and end. Include some exciting action scenes.

Outline the story below briefly.

_____
_____
_____
_____
_____

Make a list of the characters in your story.   _____
                                                                                _____
                                                                                _____
                                                                                _____

Now write a script for **one** scene in your story. Remember, you can use only dialogue to show what is happening. Write the character's name and a colon before the line of dialogue. Use the back of this paper if you need more space. When you are finished, act out the scene with some other students.

_____
_____
_____
_____
_____
_____
_____
_____
_____
_____

Name_____ **Date** _____

Let's Write   letter writing

My Hero

Whom do you admire? Is it your teacher, clergyman, or a relative? Is it a famous musician, athlete, or performer? Perhaps you admire a writer or a political leader. Write that person a fan letter, telling why you think he or she is great!

First, jot down on the lines below some admirable things the person has done. Add when and where you first learned about the person. How does the person make you feel? You don't need to write in sentences. **This first stage of writing is called *prewriting*.** You are making notes to yourself.

_____
_____
_____
_____
_____

Organize your notes into paragraphs before you write your first draft. Do you want to begin your letter by telling when you first heard or saw your hero, or would it be better first to explain why you admire the person? Make an outline of your letter on the lines below.

_____
_____
_____
_____
_____

Once you have decided on the organization of your letter, write a first draft on the back of this paper.

Your next step is to make any corrections or changes necessary. Then write your letter over on another sheet of paper. This should be the final version.

If you decide to mail your letter, ask your librarian for help in finding addresses for celebrities. Many athletes and performers can be reached through their teams or shows.

Name_____ Date_____